My First Pet

Hamsters

by Cari Meister

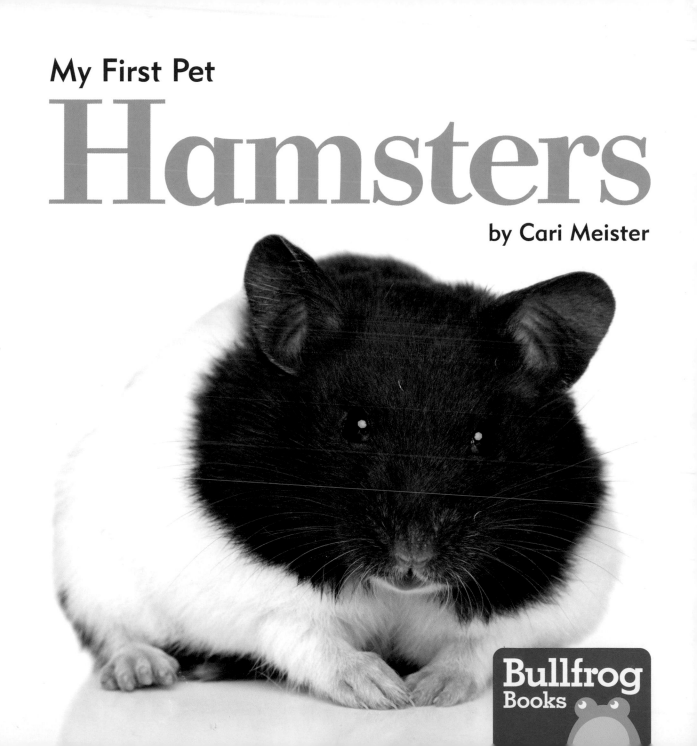

Bullfrog Books

Ideas for Parents and Teachers

Bullfrog Books let children practice reading informational text at the earliest reading levels. Repetition, familiar words, and photo labels support early readers.

Before Reading

- Ask the child to think about pet hamsters. Ask: What do you know about hamsters?
- Look at the picture glossary together. Read and discuss the words.

Read the Book

- "Walk" through the book and look at the photos. Let the child ask questions. Point out the photo labels.
- Read the book to the child, or have him or her read independently.

After Reading

- Prompt the child to think more. Ask: What do you need to take care of a hamster? Would you like to own a hamster?

Bullfrog Books are published by Jump!
5357 Penn Avenue South
Minneapolis, MN 55419
www.jumplibrary.com

Library of Congress Cataloging-in-Publication Data

Meister, Cari, author.
  Hamsters / by Cari Meister.
    pages cm. — (My first pet)
  Summary: "This photo-illustrated book for early readers tells how to take care of a pet hamster" — Provided by publisher.
  Audience: 005-008.
  Audience: K to grade 3.
  Includes bibliographical references and index.
  ISBN 978-1-62031-124-0 (hardcover) —
  ISBN 978-1-62496-191-5 (ebook) —
  ISBN 978-1-62031-146-2 (paperback)
  1. Hamsters as pets — Juvenile literature. I. Title.
SF459.H3M37 2015
636.935'6—dc23
                                    2013042370

Series Editor: Rebecca Glaser
Series Designer: Ellen Huber
Book Designer: Anna Peterson
Photo Researcher: Casie Cook

Photo Credits: Alamy/Arco Images GmbH, 6–7; Alamy/D. Hurst, 22; Alamy/Papilio, 18–19; Alamy/Top-Pet-Pics, 10–11; Getty Images/John Howard, 16–17, 23tl; iStock/Fly Fast, 13; iStock/jallfree, 12; Nature Picture Library/Aflo, 14–15, 23tr; Shutterstock/AJP, 4; Shutterstock/Andy Lidstone, 22, 24; Shutterstock/dwori, 5; Shutterstock/Elya Vatel, cover; Shutterstock/Igor Kovalchuk, 3; Shutterstock/Jagodka, 1; Shutterstock/Lepas, 20 (inset), 23br; Shutterstock/photolinc, 22; Shutterstock/Sbolotova, 22; SuperStock/Blend Images, 20–21; SuperStock/imagebroker.net, 8, 23bl; SuperStock/NaturePL, 19 (inset); Viachaslau Kraskouski, 9

Printed in the United States of America at Corporate Graphics, in North Mankato, Minnesota.
3-2014
10 9 8 7 6 5 4 3 2 1

Table of Contents

A New Pet

Azrio wants a pet.

What kind does he get?

A hamster!

5

Hammy loves his cage.

It has an exercise wheel.

He runs on it.

exercise
wheel

Sam feeds Fuzz.

hamster food

He gives him hamster food.

He gives him vegetables.

Hamsters need
fresh water.

Tia puts water
in a water bottle.

Alf drinks.

water
bottle

Eva is ready for bed.

But Rex is just waking up!

13

Hamsters are nocturnal.
They sleep during the day.
They are up at night.

hamster
ball

Lon puts Zed in a ball.

Zed runs.

He runs and runs.

He is safe in the ball.

Joe cleans Peach's cage.

He does not wash Peach.

Hamsters clean themselves.

Hamsters are cool pets!

What Does a Hamster Need?

water bottle
Hamsters need fresh water every day.

cage
A place where hamsters are kept so they can't run away.

food dish
Hamsters eat hamster food and vegetables.

exercise wheel
A plastic wheel where hamsters run in place.

Picture Glossary

hamster ball
A clear ball with air holes for hamsters to stay inside and run.

nocturnal
Awake at night and sleeping during the day.

hamster food
A mix of pellets and seeds that you can buy at pet stores.

vegetable
A food that comes from a plant; hamsters may eat vegetables.

Index

To Learn More

Learning more is as easy as 1, 2, 3.

1) Go to www.factsurfer.com

2) Enter "pet hamster" into the search box.

3) Click the "Surf" button to see a list of websites.

With factsurfer.com, finding more information is just a click away.